# Gifts from a Jar

## Cookies, Brownies & Bars

# Gift Giving Made Easy

Show your friends and family just how much you care by giving them a beautiful homemade gift jar filled with the ingredients to bake delicious cookies, brownies and bars.

Keep the following tips in mind when preparing your gift jars.

- Always use a food-safe jar or container with an airtight lid. Make sure the jar or container is completely dry before filling it with ingredients.
- Use the jar size called for in the recipe.
- Measure all the ingredients accurately.
- For ease in filling, use a wide-mouth jar if possible. Layer the ingredients into the jar using a ¼-cup dry measuring cup or the largest spoon that fits through the mouth of the jar.
- For more attractive jars, divide ingredients with large amounts (1 cup or more) into 2 layers.
- Fine ingredients such as flour and granulated sugar are best layered on the bottom of the jar, or on top of more compact ingredients, such as oats and brown sugar. When placed on top of loosely layered ingredients, such as chocolate chips or nuts, flour and granulated sugar tend to cover up those loosely layered ingredients.
- After the jar is filled make sure to replace the lid securely. Then, tear out the corresponding gift tag from this book. Cover the top of the jar with a 9- or 10-inch circle of fabric. Tie the fabric and the gift tag onto the jar with raffia, ribbon, satin cord, string, yarn or lace.

# Tangy Lemonade Bars Mix

2¼ cups all-purpose flour
1 cup sugar
1 cup dried cranberries
1 tablespoon grated lemon peel
¾ teaspoon baking soda
¾ teaspoon salt

**1.** Layer ingredients attractively in any order into 1-quart food storage jar with tight-fitting lid. Pack ingredients down slightly before adding another layer.

**2.** Cover top of jar with fabric; attach gift tag with raffia or ribbon.

*Makes one 1-quart jar*

## Tangy Lemonade Bars

**½ cup butter, softened**
**⅓ cup thawed frozen lemonade concentrate**
**1 egg**
**1 jar Tangy Lemonade Bars Mix**

**1.** Preheat oven to 375°F. Lightly grease 13×9-inch baking pan.

**2.** Beat butter in large bowl until smooth. Beat in lemonade concentrate and egg until blended. (Mixture may appear curdled.) Add bar cookie mix to butter mixture; stir until well blended.

**3.** Press dough evenly in prepared pan. Bake 20 to 25 minutes or until golden. Cool completely in pan on wire rack. Cut into bars.

*Makes 2½ dozen bars*

# Cowboy Cookie Mix

1 cup all-purpose flour
1 cup uncooked old-fashioned oats
¾ cup semisweet chocolate chips
½ cup packed light brown sugar
½ cup chopped nuts
½ cup seedless and/or golden raisins
¼ cup granulated sugar
2 tablespoons unsweetened cocoa powder
½ teaspoon baking powder
¼ teaspoon baking soda

**1.** Layer ingredients attractively in any order into 1-quart food storage jar with tight-fitting lid. Pack ingredients down slightly before adding another layer.

**2.** Cover top of jar with fabric; attach gift tag with raffia or ribbon.

*Makes one 1-quart jar*

## Cowboy Cookies

**½ cup butter, softened**
**1 egg**
**1 teaspoon vanilla**
**1 jar Cowboy Cookie Mix**

**1.** Preheat oven to 350°F. Lightly grease cookie sheets.

**2.** Beat butter in large bowl until smooth. Beat in egg and vanilla until blended. (Mixture may appear curdled.) Add cookie mix to butter mixture; stir until well blended.

**3.** Drop rounded tablespoonfuls dough 2 inches apart onto prepared cookie sheets. Bake 12 to 14 minutes or until edges are lightly browned. Remove to wire racks to cool completely.

*Makes about 2½ dozen cookies*

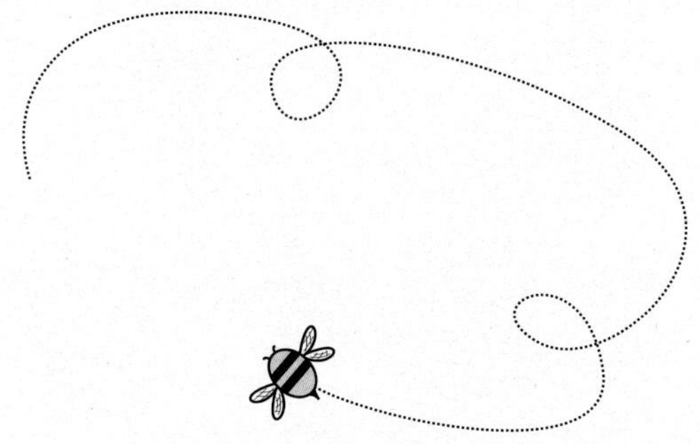

# Cocoa Brownie Mix

- 1¼ cups all-purpose flour
- 1 cup granulated sugar
- ¾ cup packed light brown sugar
- ⅔ cup unsweetened cocoa powder
- ½ cup chopped walnuts
- 1 teaspoon baking powder
- ¼ teaspoon salt

**1.** Layer ingredients attractively in any order into 1-quart food storage jar with tight-fitting lid. Pack ingredients down slightly before adding another layer.

**2.** Cover top of jar with fabric; attach gift tag with raffia or ribbon.

*Makes one 1-quart jar*

# Cocoa Brownies

¾ cup butter, softened
3 eggs
1½ teaspoons vanilla
1 jar Cocoa Brownie Mix

1. Preheat oven to 350°F. Lightly grease 13×9-inch baking pan.

2. Beat butter in large bowl until smooth. Beat in eggs and vanilla until blended. (Mixture may appear curdled.) Add brownie mix to butter mixture; stir until well blended.

3. Spread batter evenly in prepared pan. Bake 20 to 25 minutes or until brownies spring back when lightly touched. Do not overbake. Cool in pan on wire rack.

*Makes 2½ dozen brownies*

# Fruit & Oat Squares Mix

- 2 cups all-purpose flour
- 2 cups uncooked quick oats
- 1½ cups packed light brown sugar
- 1 teaspoon baking soda
- ½ teaspoon salt
- ½ teaspoon ground cinnamon

**1.** Layer ingredients attractively in any order into 1½-quart food storage jar with tight-fitting lid. Pack ingredients down slightly before adding another layer.

**2.** Cover top of jar with fabric; attach gift tag with raffia or ribbon.

*Makes one 1½-quart jar*

# Fruit & Oat Squares

**1 jar Fruit & Oat Squares Mix**
**⅔ cup butter, softened**
**1½ cups apricot, cherry or other fruit flavor preserves**

**1.** Preheat oven to 350°F. Lightly grease 13×9-inch baking pan.

**2.** Place bar cookie mix in large bowl; mix well. Add butter; stir with fork until mixture is crumbly.

**3.** Reserve 1 cup crumb mixture for topping. Press remaining crumb mixture onto bottom of prepared pan. Bake 7 to 8 minutes or until lightly browned.

**4.** Spread preserves over crust; sprinkle with reserved crumb mixture. Bake 23 to 25 minutes or until topping is golden brown. Cool completely in pan on wire rack. *Makes 2 dozen bars*

# Chocolate-Coconut-Toffee Delights Mix

- 1 package (12 ounces) semisweet chocolate chips, divided
- 1½ cups flaked coconut
- 1 cup toffee baking pieces
- ¾ cup packed light brown sugar
- ½ cup all-purpose flour
- ¼ teaspoon baking powder
- ¼ teaspoon salt

**1.** Place 1 cup chocolate chips in resealable plastic food storage bag; seal bag. Layer all remaining ingredients attractively in any order into 1½-quart food storage jar with tight-fitting lid. Pack ingredients down slightly before adding another layer. Use chocolate chips in bag as final layer in jar.

**2.** Cover top of jar with fabric; attach gift tag with raffia or ribbon.

*Makes one 1½-quart jar*

# Chocolate-Coconut-Toffee Delights

**1 jar Chocolate-Coconut-Toffee Delights Mix**
**¼ cup butter, cut into small pieces**
**2 eggs**
**1 teaspoon vanilla**

**1.** Preheat oven to 350°F. Line cookie sheets with parchment paper. Place 1 cup chocolate chips from bag in large microwavable bowl. Microwave at HIGH 1 minute; stir. Microwave 30 to 60 seconds or until chips are melted; stir well.

**2.** Add butter to chocolate in bowl; stir until melted. Beat in eggs and vanilla until blended. Add remaining cookie mix to chocolate mixture; stir until blended.

**3.** Drop heaping ⅓ cupfuls dough 3 inches apart onto prepared cookie sheets. Flatten dough into 3½-inch rounds. Bake about 15 minutes or until edges are just firm to the touch. Let cookies stand on cookie sheets 2 minutes. Slide parchment paper and cookies onto countertop; cool. *Makes 1 dozen (5-inch) cookies*

# Mystical Bars Mix

**1 cup graham cracker crumbs**
**1 cup coarsely chopped pecans**
**¾ cup flaked coconut**
**¾ cup semisweet chocolate chips**
**½ cup uncooked old-fashioned or quick oats**
**½ cup raisins**

**1.** Layer ingredients attractively in any order into 1-quart food storage jar with tight-fitting lid. Pack ingredients down slightly before adding another layer.

**2.** Cover top of jar with fabric; attach gift tag with raffia or ribbon.

*Makes one 1-quart jar*

# Mystical Bars

**⅓ cup butter**
**1 jar Mystical Bars Mix**
**1 can (14 ounces) sweetened condensed milk**

**1.** Preheat oven to 350°F. Melt butter in 13×9-inch baking pan. Remove from oven.

**2.** Place bar cookie mix in large bowl. Add sweetened condensed milk; stir with spoon until well blended.

**3.** Spread batter evenly in prepared pan. Bake 22 to 25 minutes or until lightly browned. Cool in pan on wire rack 5 minutes. Cut into bars. Cool completely in pan on wire rack.

*Makes 2½ dozen bars*

# Oatmeal Candied Chippers Mix

2¾ cups uncooked old-fashioned or quick oats
¾ cup granulated sugar
¾ cup all-purpose flour
¾ cup packed light brown sugar
¾ cup candy-coated semisweet chocolate chips or candy-coated chocolate pieces
¾ teaspoon salt
½ teaspoon baking soda

**1.** Layer ingredients attractively in any order into 1½-quart food storage jar with tight-fitting lid. Pack ingredients down slightly before adding another layer.

**2.** Cover top of jar with fabric; attach gift tag with raffia or ribbon.

*Makes one 1½-quart jar*

# Oatmeal Candied Chippers

- ¾ cup butter, softened
- 3 tablespoons milk
- 1 egg
- 2 teaspoons vanilla
- 1 jar Oatmeal Candied Chippers Mix

**1.** Preheat oven to 375°F. Lightly grease cookie sheets.

**2.** Beat butter in large bowl until smooth. Beat in milk, egg and vanilla until blended. (Mixture may appear curdled.) Add cookie mix to butter mixture; stir until well blended.

**3.** Drop rounded tablespoonfuls dough 2 inches apart onto prepared cookie sheets. Bake 10 to 12 minutes or until edges are golden brown. Let cookies stand on cookie sheets 2 minutes. Remove cookies to wire racks to cool completely.

*Makes about 4 dozen cookies*

## Fruit & Oat Squares

**1 jar Fruit & Oat Squares Mix**
**2/3 cup butter, softened**
**1½ cups apricot, cherry or other fruit flavor preserves**

**1.** Preheat oven to 350°F. Lightly grease 13×9-inch baking pan.
**2.** Place bar cookie mix in large bowl; mix well. Add butter; stir with fork until mixture is crumbly.
**3.** Reserve 1 cup crumb mixture for topping. Press remaining crumb mixture onto bottom of prepared pan. Bake 7 to 8 minutes or until lightly browned.
**4.** Spread preserves over crust; sprinkle with reserved crumb mixture. Bake 23 to 25 minutes or until topping is golden brown. Cool completely in pan on wire rack.

*Makes 2 dozen bars*

## Cocoa Brownies

**3/4 cup butter, softened**
**3 eggs**
**1½ teaspoons vanilla**
**1 jar Cocoa Brownie Mix**

**1.** Preheat oven to 350°F. Lightly grease 13×9-inch baking pan.
**2.** Beat butter in large bowl until smooth. Beat in eggs and vanilla until blended. (Mixture may appear curdled.) Add brownie mix to butter mixture; stir until well blended.
**3.** Spread batter evenly in prepared pan. Bake 20 to 25 minutes or until brownies spring back when lightly touched. Do not overbake. Cool in pan on wire rack.

*Makes 2½ dozen brownies*

## Fruit & Oat Squares

**1 jar Fruit & Oat Squares Mix**
**2/3 cup butter, softened**
**1½ cups apricot, cherry or other fruit flavor preserves**

**1.** Preheat oven to 350°F. Lightly grease 13×9-inch baking pan.
**2.** Place bar cookie mix in large bowl; mix well. Add butter; stir with fork until mixture is crumbly.
**3.** Reserve 1 cup crumb mixture for topping. Press remaining crumb mixture onto bottom of prepared pan. Bake 7 to 8 minutes or until lightly browned.
**4.** Spread preserves over crust; sprinkle with reserved crumb mixture. Bake 23 to 25 minutes or until topping is golden brown. Cool completely in pan on wire rack.

*Makes 2 dozen bars*

## Cocoa Brownies

**3/4 cup butter, softened**
**3 eggs**
**1½ teaspoons vanilla**
**1 jar Cocoa Brownie Mix**

**1.** Preheat oven to 350°F. Lightly grease 13×9-inch baking pan.
**2.** Beat butter in large bowl until smooth. Beat in eggs and vanilla until blended. (Mixture may appear curdled.) Add brownie mix to butter mixture; stir until well blended.
**3.** Spread batter evenly in prepared pan. Bake 20 to 25 minutes or until brownies spring back when lightly touched. Do not overbake. Cool in pan on wire rack.

*Makes 2½ dozen brownies*

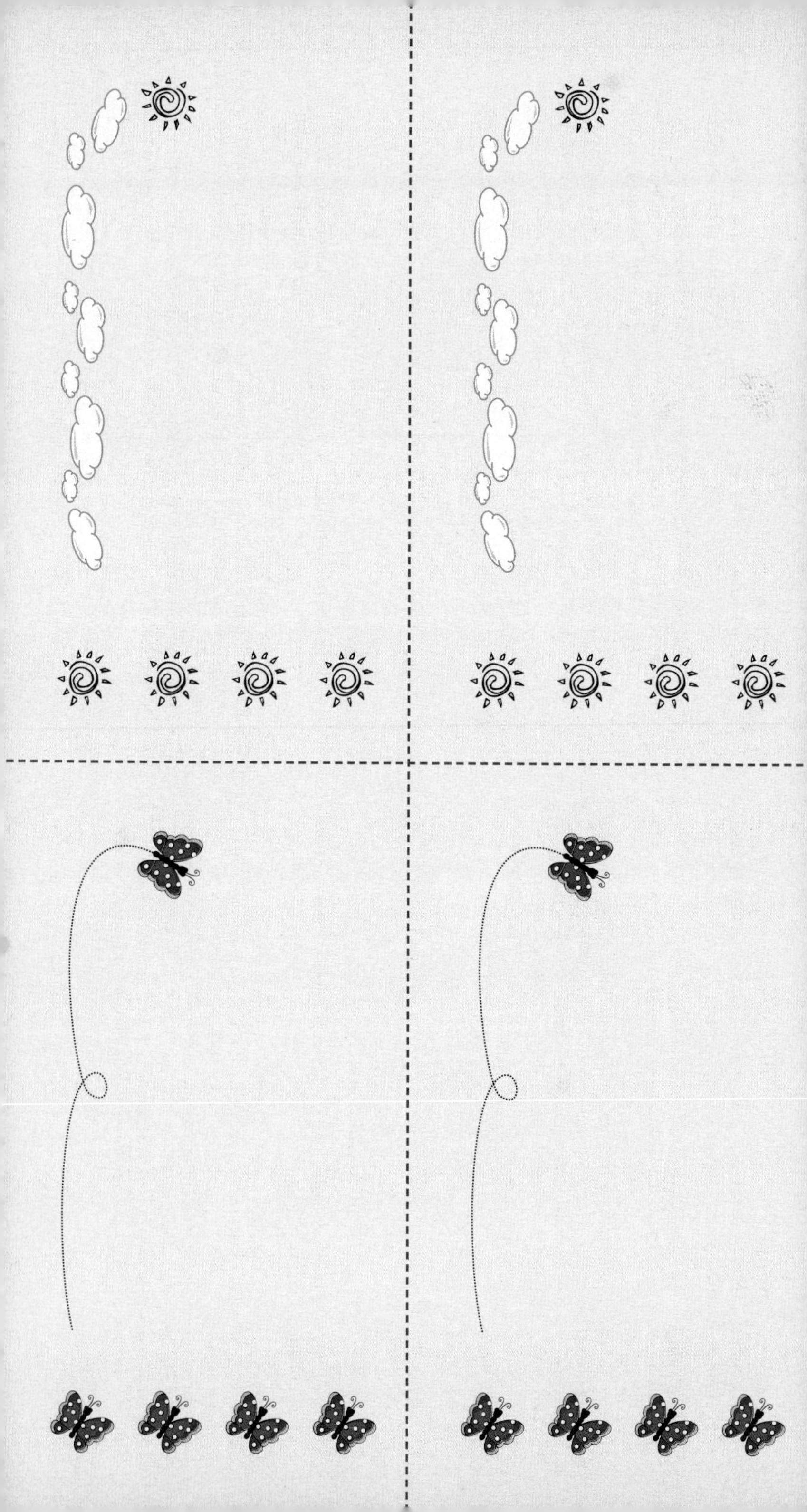

## Mystical Bars

**⅓ cup butter**
**1 jar Mystical Bars Mix**
**1 can (14 ounces) sweetened condensed milk**

**1.** Preheat oven to 350°F. Melt butter in 13×9-inch baking pan. Remove from oven.
**2.** Place bar cookie mix in large bowl. Add sweetened condensed milk; stir with spoon until well blended.
**3.** Spread batter evenly in prepared pan. Bake 22 to 25 minutes or until lightly browned. Cool in pan on wire rack 5 minutes. Cut into bars. Cool completely in pan on wire rack.

*Makes 2½ dozen bars*

## Chocolate-Coconut-Toffee Delights

**1 jar Chocolate-Coconut-Toffee Delights Mix**
**¼ cup butter, cut into pieces**
**2 eggs**
**1 teaspoon vanilla**

**1.** Preheat oven to 350°F. Line cookie sheets with parchment paper. Place 1 cup chocolate chips from bag in large microwavable bowl. Microwave at HIGH 1 minute; stir. Microwave 30 to 60 seconds or until chips are melted; stir well.
**2.** Add butter to chocolate in bowl; stir until melted. Beat in eggs and vanilla until blended. Add remaining cookie mix to chocolate mixture; stir until blended.
**3.** Drop heaping ⅓ cupfuls dough 3 inches apart onto prepared cookie sheets. Flatten dough into 3½-inch rounds. Bake about 15 minutes or until edges are just firm to the touch. Let cookies stand on cookie sheets 2 minutes. Slide parchment paper and cookies onto countertop; cool.

*Makes 1 dozen (5-inch) cookies*

## Mystical Bars

**⅓ cup butter**
**1 jar Mystical Bars Mix**
**1 can (14 ounces) sweetened condensed milk**

**1.** Preheat oven to 350°F. Melt butter in 13×9-inch baking pan. Remove from oven.
**2.** Place bar cookie mix in large bowl. Add sweetened condensed milk; stir with spoon until well blended.
**3.** Spread batter evenly in prepared pan. Bake 22 to 25 minutes or until lightly browned. Cool in pan on wire rack 5 minutes. Cut into bars. Cool completely in pan on wire rack.

*Makes 2½ dozen bars*

## Chocolate-Coconut-Toffee Delights

**1 jar Chocolate-Coconut-Toffee Delights Mix**
**¼ cup butter, cut into pieces**
**2 eggs**
**1 teaspoon vanilla**

**1.** Preheat oven to 350°F. Line cookie sheets with parchment paper. Place 1 cup chocolate chips from bag in large microwavable bowl. Microwave at HIGH 1 minute; stir. Microwave 30 to 60 seconds or until chips are melted; stir well.
**2.** Add butter to chocolate in bowl; stir until melted. Beat in eggs and vanilla until blended. Add remaining cookie mix to chocolate mixture; stir until blended.
**3.** Drop heaping ⅓ cupfuls dough 3 inches apart onto prepared cookie sheets. Flatten dough into 3½-inch rounds. Bake about 15 minutes or until edges are just firm to the touch. Let cookies stand on cookie sheets 2 minutes. Slide parchment paper and cookies onto countertop; cool.

*Makes 1 dozen (5-inch) cookies*

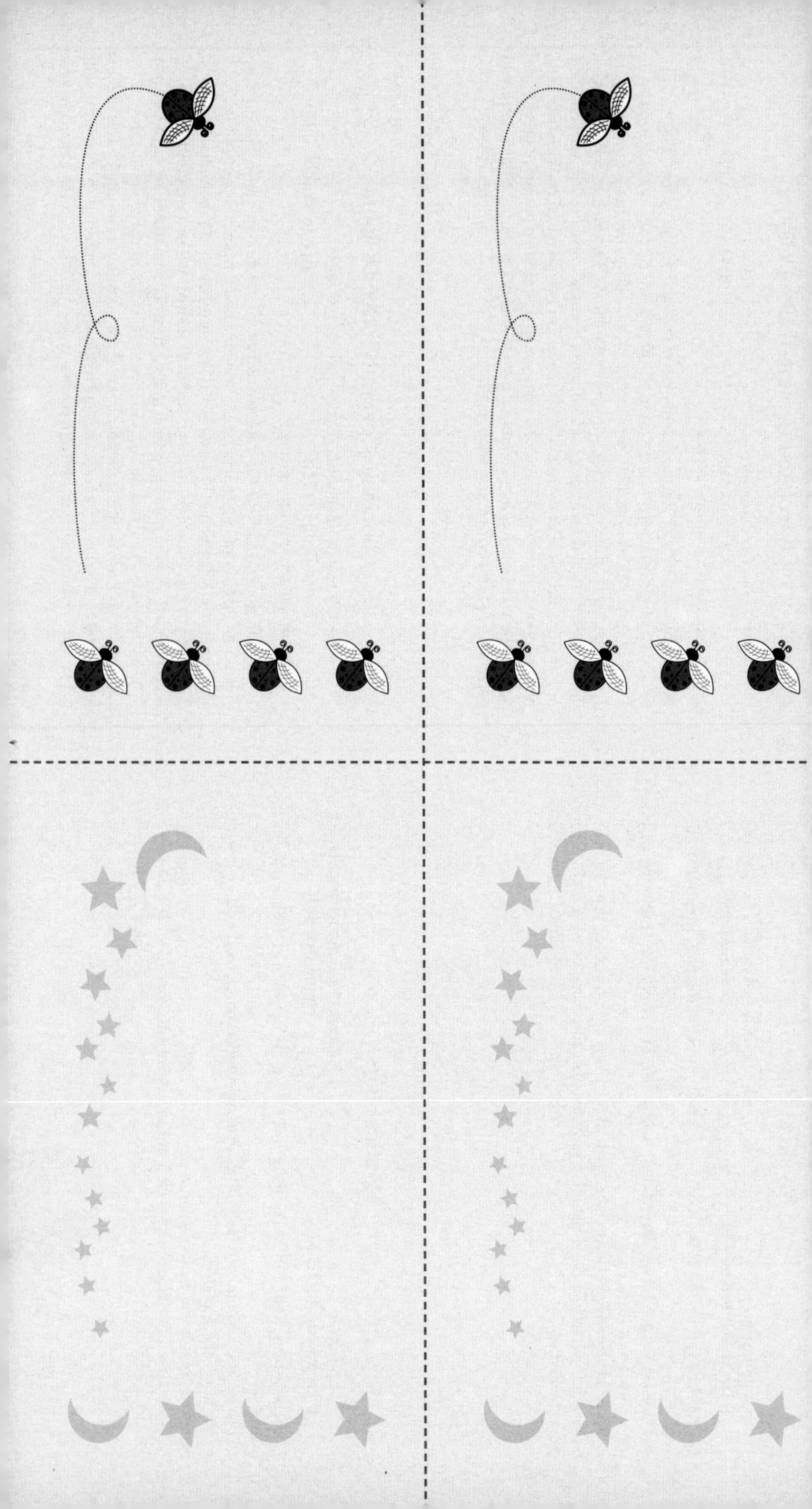

## Rocky Road Brownies

**1 jar Rocky Road Brownie Mix**
**½ cup butter, melted**
**¼ cup buttermilk**
**1 egg**
**1 teaspoon vanilla**

**1.** Preheat oven to 350°F. Lightly grease 8×8-inch baking pan. Remove marshmallows from plastic food storage bag in jar; set aside.
**2.** Place remaining brownie mix in large bowl. Add melted butter, buttermilk, egg and vanilla; stir until well blended.
**3.** Spread batter evenly in prepared pan. Bake 25 to 30 minutes or until set. Sprinkle with reserved marshmallows. Bake 3 to 5 minutes or until marshmallows are puffed and slightly melted. Cool in pan on wire rack.

*Makes 16 brownies*

## Oatmeal Candied Chippers

**¾ cup butter, softened**
**3 tablespoons milk**
**1 egg**
**2 teaspoons vanilla**
**1 jar Oatmeal Candied Chippers Mix**

**1.** Preheat oven to 375°F. Lightly grease cookie sheets.
**2.** Beat butter in large bowl until smooth. Beat in milk, egg and vanilla until blended. (Mixture may appear curdled.) Add cookie mix to butter mixture; stir until well blended.
**3.** Drop rounded tablespoonfuls dough 2 inches apart onto prepared cookie sheets. Bake 10 to 12 minutes or until edges are golden brown. Let cookies stand on cookie sheets 2 minutes. Remove cookies to wire racks to cool completely.

*Makes about 4 dozen cookies*


## Oatmeal Candied Chippers

**¾ cup butter, softened**
**3 tablespoons milk**
**1 egg**
**2 teaspoons vanilla**
**1 jar Oatmeal Candied Chippers Mix**

**1.** Preheat oven to 375°F. Lightly grease cookie sheets.
**2.** Beat butter in large bowl until smooth. Beat in milk, egg and vanilla until blended. (Mixture may appear curdled.) Add cookie mix to butter mixture; stir until well blended.
**3.** Drop rounded tablespoonfuls dough 2 inches apart onto prepared cookie sheets. Bake 10 to 12 minutes or until edges are golden brown. Let cookies stand on cookie sheets 2 minutes. Remove cookies to wire racks to cool completely.

*Makes about 4 dozen cookies*

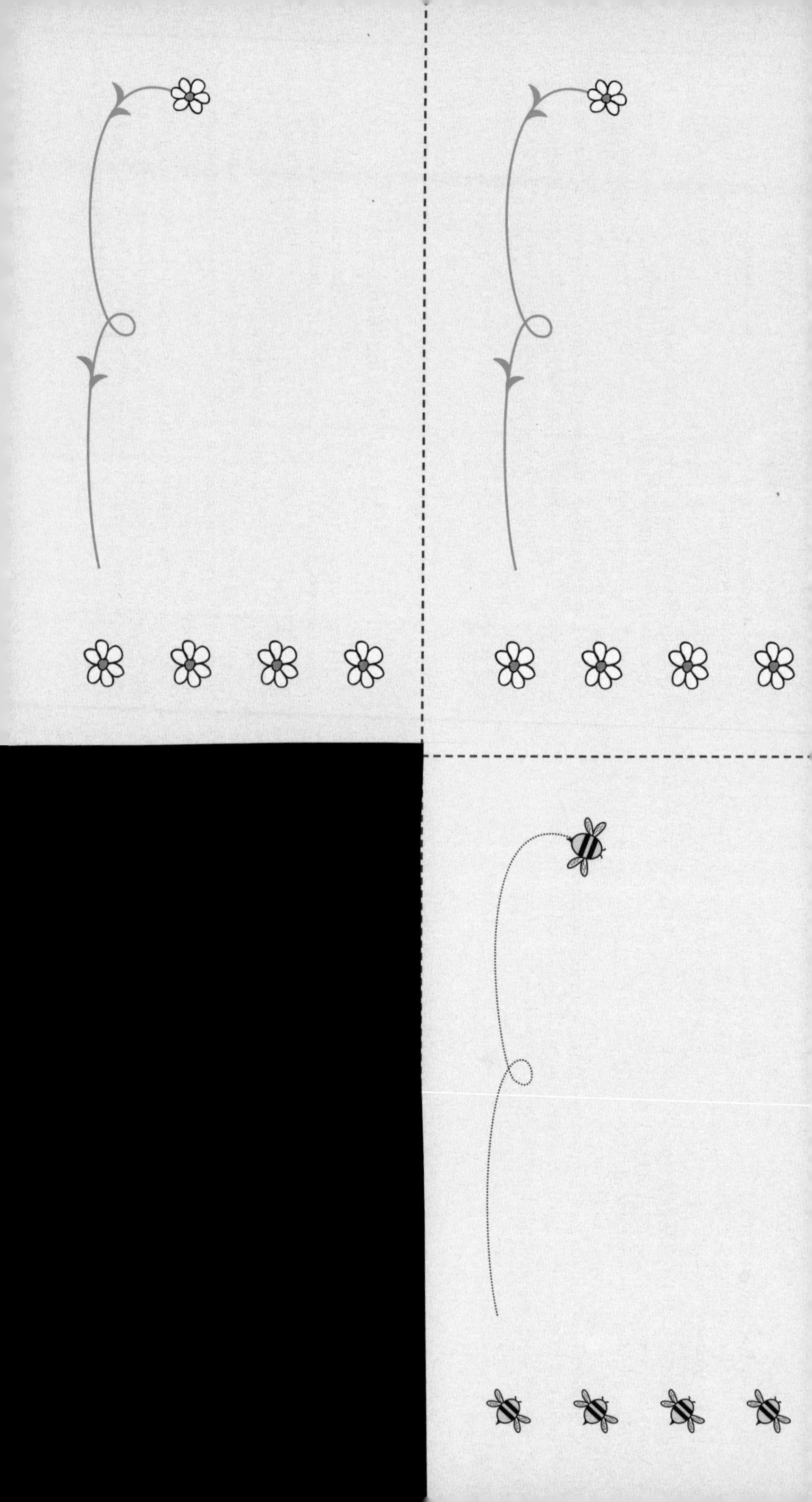

## No-Fuss Bar Cookies

**1 jar No-Fuss Bar Cookie Mix**

**1 can (14 ounces) sweetened condensed milk**

**1.** Preheat oven to 350°F. Lightly grease 13×9-inch baking pan.

**2.** Place bar cookie mix in large bowl. Add sweetened condensed milk; stir with spoon until well blended.

**3.** Spread batter evenly in prepared pan. Bake 15 to 18 minutes or until edges are golden brown. Cool completely in pan on wire rack.

*Makes 2 dozen bars*

## Orange Walnut Chip Cookies

**½ cup butter, softened**

**1 egg**

**1 jar Orange Walnut Chip Cookie Mix**

**1.** Preheat oven to 375°F. Lightly grease cookie sheets.

**2.** Beat butter in large bowl until smooth. Beat in egg until blended. (Mixture may appear curdled.) Add cookie mix to butter mixture; stir until well blended.

**3.** Drop rounded teaspoonfuls dough 2 inches apart onto prepared cookie sheets. Bake 8 to 10 minutes or until edges are golden brown. Let cookies stand on cookie sheets 2 minutes. Remove cookies to wire racks to cool completely.

*Makes 3½ dozen cookies*


## Orange Walnut Chip Cookies

**½ cup butter, softened**

**1 egg**

**1 jar Orange Walnut Chip Cookie Mix**

**1.** Preheat oven to 375°F. Lightly grease cookie sheets.

**2.** Beat butter in large bowl until smooth. Beat in egg until blended. (Mixture may appear curdled.) Add cookie mix to butter mixture; stir until well blended.

**3.** Drop rounded teaspoonfuls dough 2 inches apart onto prepared cookie sheets. Bake 8 to 10 minutes or until edges are golden brown. Let cookies stand on cookie sheets 2 minutes. Remove cookies to wire racks to cool completely.

*Makes 3½ dozen cookies*

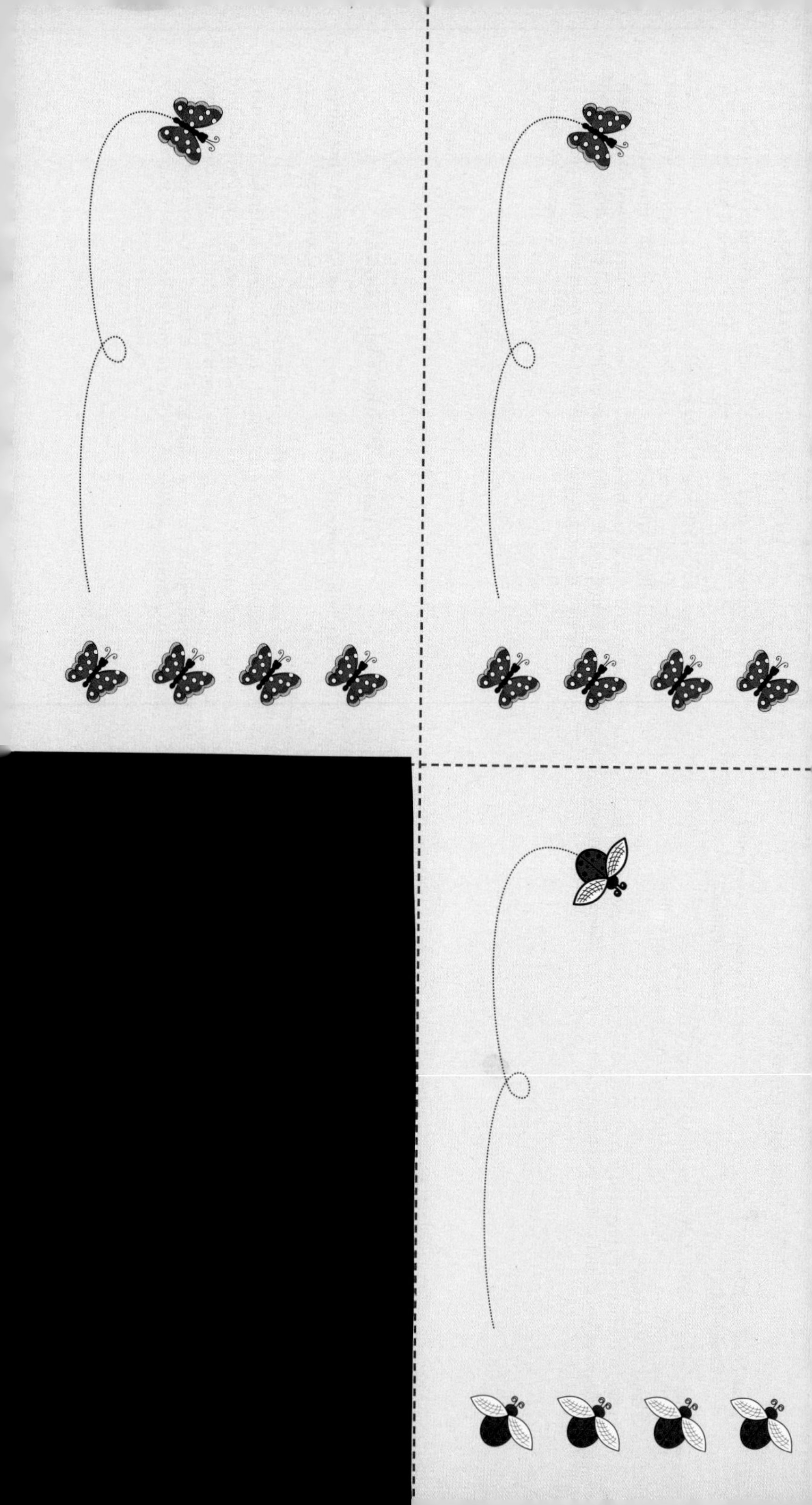

## Strawberry Oat Bars

- **1 cup butter, softened**
- **1 jar Strawberry Oat Bars Mix**
- **1 can (21 ounces) strawberry pie filling**
- **¾ teaspoon almond extract**

**1.** Preheat oven to 375°F.
**2.** Beat butter in large bowl until smooth. Add bar cookie mix to butter; beat until well blended and crumbly.
**3.** Press ⅔ of crumb mixture onto bottom of ungreased 13×9-inch baking pan. Bake 15 minutes; let cool 5 minutes on wire rack.
**4.** Place pie filling in food processor; process until smooth. Stir in almond extract.
**5.** Pour filling mixture over crust. Sprinkle remaining crumb mixture evenly over filling. Return pan to oven; bake 20 to 25 minutes or until topping is golden and filling is slightly bubbly. Cool completely on wire rack.

*Makes 2½ dozen bars*

## Rum Fruitcake Cookies

- **⅓ cup shortening**
- **2 eggs**
- **3 tablespoons orange juice**
- **1½ teaspoons rum extract**
- **1 jar Rum Fruitcake Cookie Mix**

**1.** Preheat oven to 375°F. Lightly grease cookie sheets.
**2.** Beat shortening in large bowl until smooth. Beat in eggs, orange juice and rum extract until blended. (Mixture may appear curdled.) Add cookie mix to shortening mixture; stir until well blended.
**3.** Drop rounded teaspoonfuls dough 2 inches apart onto prepared cookie sheets. Bake 11 to 13 minutes or until golden. Do not overbake. Let cookies stand on cookie sheets 2 minutes. Remove cookies to wire racks to cool completely.

*Makes 3 dozen cookies*


## Strawberry Oat Bars

- **1 cup butter, softened**
- **1 jar Strawberry Oat Bars Mix**
- **1 can (21 ounces) strawberry pie filling**
- **¾ teaspoon almond extract**

**1.** Preheat oven to 375°F.
**2.** Beat butter in large bowl until smooth. Add bar cookie mix to butter; beat until well blended and crumbly.
**3.** Press ⅔ of crumb mixture onto bottom of ungreased 13×9-inch baking pan. Bake 15 minutes; let cool 5 minutes on wire rack.
**4.** Place pie filling in food processor; process until smooth. Stir in almond extract.
**5.** Pour filling mixture over crust. Sprinkle remaining crumb mixture evenly over filling. Return pan to oven; bake 20 to 25 minutes or until topping is golden and filling is slightly bubbly. Cool completely on wire rack.

*Makes 2½ dozen bars*



## Rum Fruitcake Cookies

- **⅓ cup shortening**
- **2 eggs**
- **3 tablespoons orange juice**
- **1½ teaspoons rum extract**
- **1 jar Rum Fruitcake Cookie Mix**

**1.** Preheat oven to 375°F. Lightly grease cookie sheets.
**2.** Beat shortening in large bowl until smooth. Beat in eggs, orange juice and rum extract until blended. (Mixture may appear curdled.) Add cookie mix to shortening mixture; stir until well blended.
**3.** Drop rounded teaspoonfuls dough 2 inches apart onto prepared cookie sheets. Bake 11 to 13 minutes or until golden. Do not overbake. Let cookies stand on cookie sheets 2 minutes. Remove cookies to wire racks to cool completely.

*Makes 3 dozen cookies*

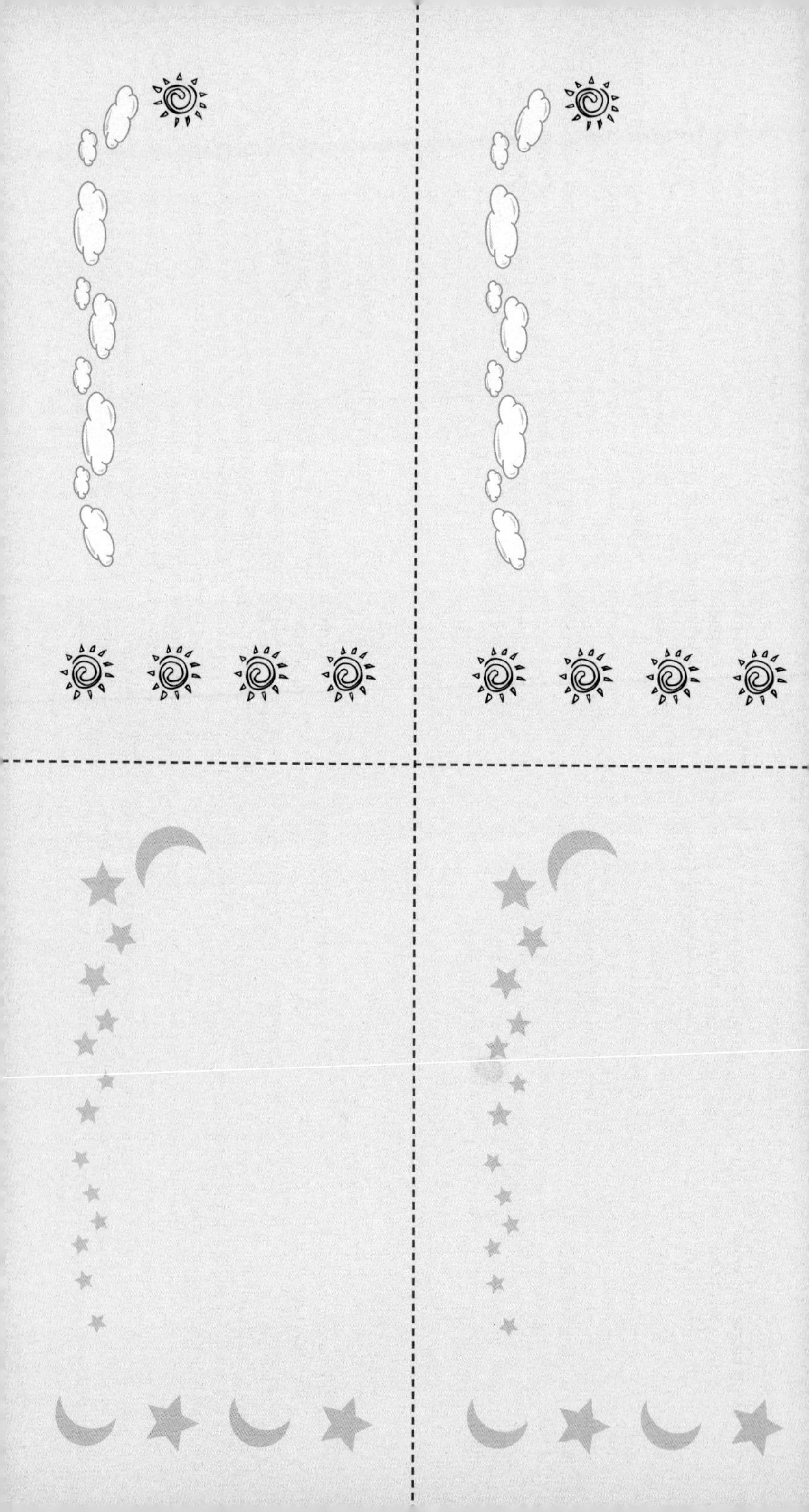

## Fabulous Blondies

**⅔ cup butter, softened**
**2 eggs**
**2 teaspoons vanilla**
**1 jar Fabulous Blondies Mix**

**1.** Preheat oven to 350°F. Lightly grease 13×9-inch baking pan.
**2.** Beat butter in large bowl until smooth. Beat in eggs and vanilla until blended. (Mixture may appear curdled.) Add blondie mix to butter mixture; stir until well blended.
**3.** Spread batter evenly in prepared pan. Bake 30 to 35 minutes or until golden brown. Cool in pan on wire rack.

*Makes 2½ dozen blondies*

## Super Chocolate Cookies

**⅔ cup butter, softened**
**2 eggs**
**1½ teaspoons vanilla**
**1 jar Super Chocolate Cookie Mix**

**1.** Preheat oven to 350°F.
**2.** Beat butter in large bowl until smooth. Beat in eggs and vanilla until blended. (Mixture may appear curdled.) Add cookie mix to butter mixture; stir until well blended.
**3.** Drop heaping tablespoonfuls dough 2 inches apart onto ungreased cookie sheets. Bake 11 to 12 minutes or until almost set. Let cookies stand on cookie sheets 2 minutes. Remove cookies to wire racks to cool completely.

*Makes 2 dozen cookies*

## Fabulous Blondies

**⅔ cup butter, softened**
**2 eggs**
**2 teaspoons vanilla**
**1 jar Fabulous Blondies Mix**

**1.** Preheat oven to 350°F. Lightly grease 13×9-inch baking pan.
**2.** Beat butter in large bowl until smooth. Beat in eggs and vanilla until blended. (Mixture may appear curdled.) Add blondie mix to butter mixture; stir until well blended.
**3.** Spread batter evenly in prepared pan. Bake 30 to 35 minutes or until golden brown. Cool in pan on wire rack.

*Makes 2½ dozen blondies*

## Super Chocolate Cookies

**⅔ cup butter, softened**
**2 eggs**
**1½ teaspoons vanilla**
**1 jar Super Chocolate Cookie Mix**

**1.** Preheat oven to 350°F.
**2.** Beat butter in large bowl until smooth. Beat in eggs and vanilla until blended. (Mixture may appear curdled.) Add cookie mix to butter mixture; stir until well blended.
**3.** Drop heaping tablespoonfuls dough 2 inches apart onto ungreased cookie sheets. Bake 11 to 12 minutes or until almost set. Let cookies stand on cookie sheets 2 minutes. Remove cookies to wire racks to cool completely.

*Makes 2 dozen cookies*

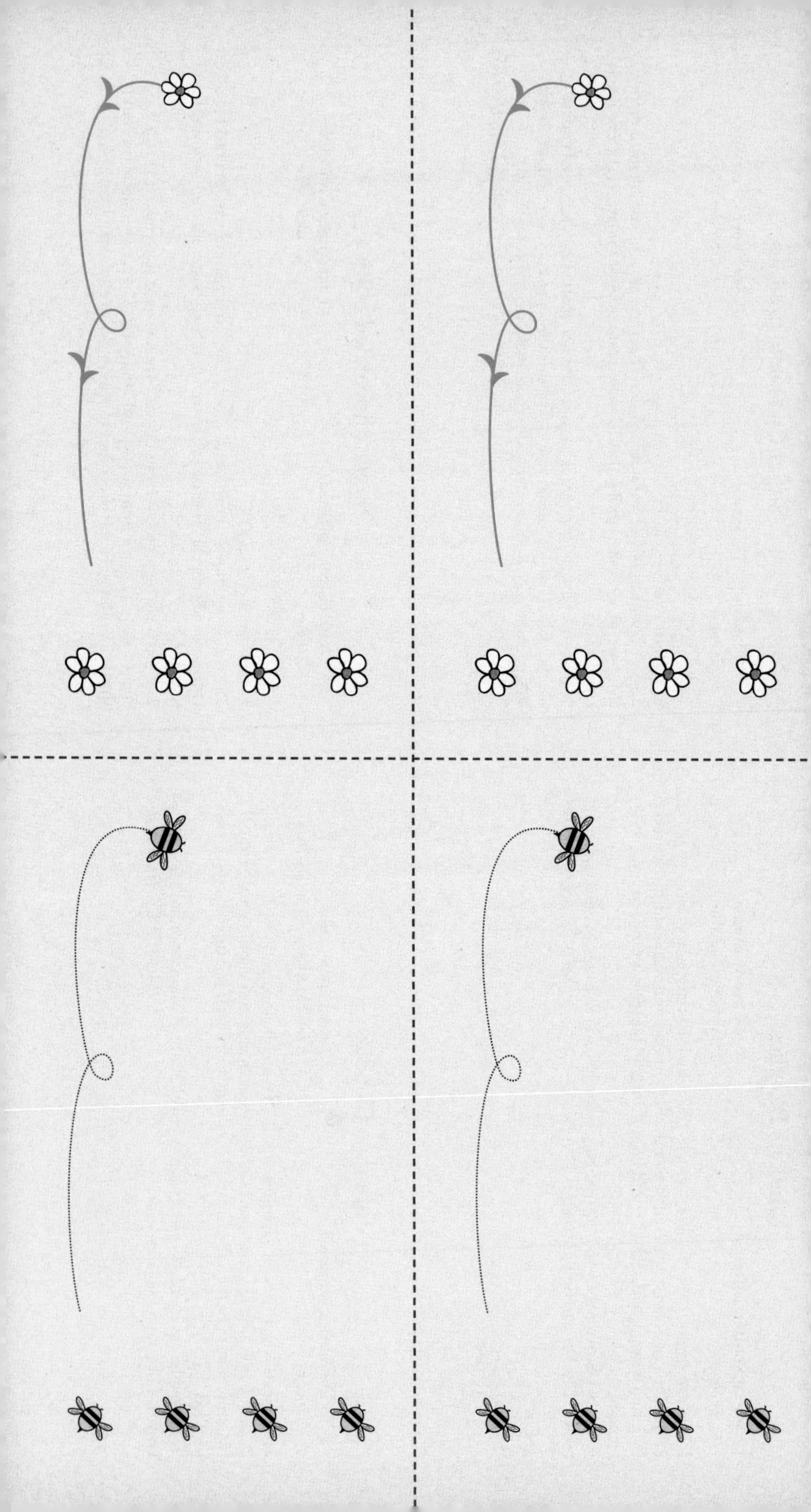

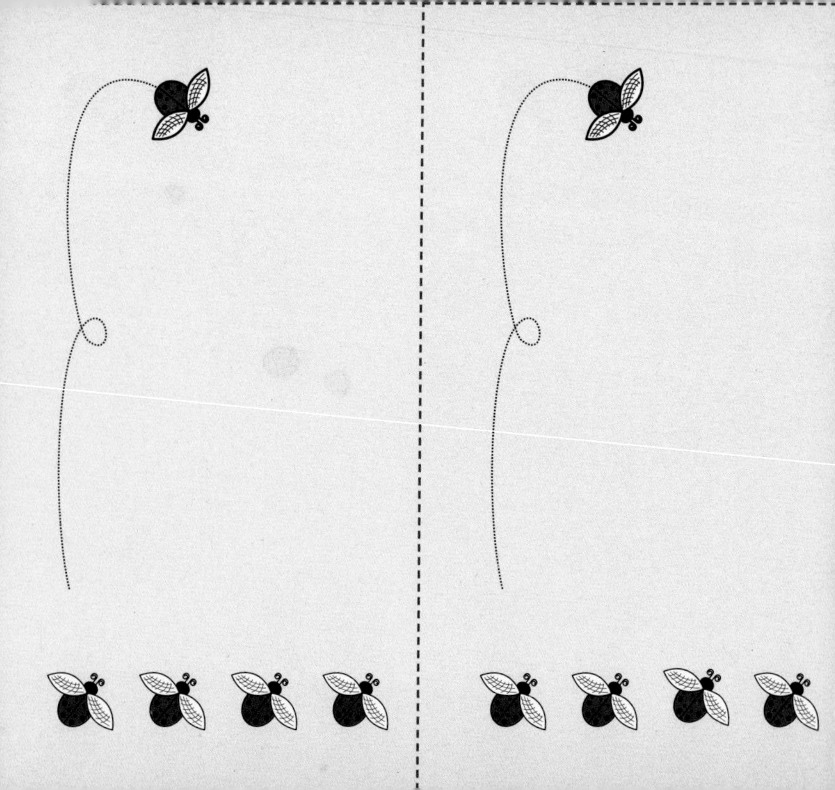

# Rocky Road Brownie Mix

- 1 cup sugar
- 1 cup semisweet chocolate chips
- ¾ cup coarsely chopped walnuts
- ½ cup all-purpose flour
- ½ cup unsweetened cocoa powder
- 1 cup miniature marshmallows

**1.** Layer all ingredients except marshmallows attractively in any order into 1-quart food storage jar with tight-fitting lid. Pack ingredients down slightly before adding another layer. Place marshmallows in resealable plastic food storage bag; seal bag. Use marshmallows as final layer in jar.

**2.** Cover top of jar with fabric; attach gift tag with raffia or ribbon.

*Makes one 1-quart jar*

# Rocky Road Brownies

1 jar Rocky Road Brownie Mix
½ cup butter, melted
¼ cup buttermilk
1 egg
1 teaspoon vanilla

**1.** Preheat oven to 350°F. Lightly grease 8×8-inch baking pan. Remove marshmallows from plastic food storage bag in jar; set aside.

**2.** Place remaining brownie mix in large bowl. Add melted butter, buttermilk, egg and vanilla; stir until well blended.

**3.** Spread batter evenly in prepared pan. Bake 25 to 30 minutes or until set. Sprinkle with reserved marshmallows. Bake 3 to 5 minutes or until marshmallows are puffed and slightly melted. Cool in pan on wire rack. *Makes 16 brownies*

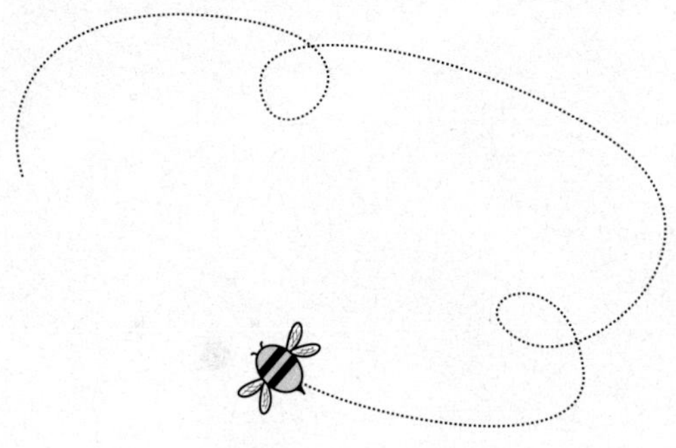

# Orange Walnut Chip Cookie Mix

- 1½ cups uncooked old-fashioned oats
- 1 cup packed light brown sugar
- 1 cup semisweet chocolate chips
- ½ cup all-purpose flour
- ½ cup coarsely chopped walnuts
- 1 tablespoon grated orange peel
- ¼ teaspoon salt
- ¼ teaspoon baking soda

**1.** Layer ingredients attractively in any order into 1-quart food storage jar with tight-fitting lid. Pack ingredients down slightly before adding another layer.

**2.** Cover top of jar with fabric; attach gift tag with raffia or ribbon.

*Makes one 1-quart jar*

# Orange Walnut Chip Cookies

- **½ cup butter, softened**
- **1 egg**
- **1 jar Orange Walnut Chip Cookie Mix**

**1.** Preheat oven to 375°F. Lightly grease cookie sheets.

**2.** Beat butter in large bowl until smooth. Beat in egg until blended. (Mixture may appear curdled.) Add cookie mix to butter mixture; stir until well blended.

**3.** Drop rounded teaspoonfuls dough 2 inches apart onto prepared cookie sheets. Bake 8 to 10 minutes or until edges are golden brown. Let cookies stand on cookie sheets 2 minutes. Remove cookies to wire racks to cool completely.

*Makes 3½ dozen cookies*

# No-Fuss Bar Cookie Mix

- 2 cups graham cracker crumbs
- 1 cup flaked coconut
- 1 cup semisweet chocolate chips
- ½ cup coarsely chopped walnuts

**1.** Layer ingredients attractively in any order into 1-quart food storage jar with tight-fitting lid. Pack ingredients down slightly before adding another layer.

**2.** Cover top of jar with fabric; attach gift tag with raffia or ribbon.

*Makes one 1-quart jar*

# No-Fuss Bar Cookies

**1 jar No-Fuss Bar Cookie Mix**
**1 can (14 ounces) sweetened condensed milk**

**1.** Preheat oven to 350°F. Lightly grease 13×9-inch baking pan.

**2.** Place bar cookie mix in large bowl. Add sweetened condensed milk; stir with spoon until well blended.

**3.** Spread batter evenly in prepared pan. Bake 15 to 18 minutes or until edges are golden brown. Cool completely in pan on wire rack.

*Makes 2 dozen bars*

# Rum Fruitcake Cookie Mix

1½ cups all-purpose flour
1 cup (4 ounces) chopped candied mixed fruit
½ cup sugar
½ cup nuts, coarsely chopped
½ cup raisins
1 teaspoon baking powder
½ teaspoon salt
½ teaspoon baking soda

**1.** Layer ingredients attractively in any order into 1-quart food storage jar with tight-fitting lid. Pack ingredients down slightly before adding another layer.

**2.** Cover top of jar with fabric; attach gift tag with raffia or ribbon.

*Makes one 1-quart jar*

# Rum Fruitcake Cookies

⅓ cup shortening
2 eggs
3 tablespoons orange juice
1½ teaspoons rum extract
1 jar Rum Fruitcake Cookie Mix

**1.** Preheat oven to 375°F. Lightly grease cookie sheets.

**2.** Beat shortening in large bowl until smooth. Beat in eggs, orange juice and rum extract until blended. (Mixture may appear curdled.) Add cookie mix to shortening mixture; stir until well blended.

**3.** Drop rounded teaspoonfuls dough 2 inches apart onto prepared cookie sheets. Bake 11 to 13 minutes or until golden. Do not overbake. Let cookies stand on cookie sheets 2 minutes. Remove cookies to wire racks to cool completely. *Makes 3 dozen cookies*

## Strawberry Oat Bars Mix

- 2¼ cups uncooked quick oats
- 1 cup all-purpose flour
- 1 cup packed light brown sugar
- 2 teaspoons baking soda
- ½ teaspoon ground cinnamon
- ¼ teaspoon salt

**1.** Layer ingredients attractively in any order into 1-quart food storage jar with tight-fitting lid. Pack ingredients down slightly before adding another layer.

**2.** Cover top of jar with fabric; attach gift tag with raffia or ribbon.

*Makes one 1-quart jar*

# Strawberry Oat Bars

1 cup butter, softened
1 jar Strawberry Oat Bars Mix
1 can (21 ounces) strawberry pie filling
¾ teaspoon almond extract

1. Preheat oven to 375°F.

2. Beat butter in large bowl until smooth. Add bar cookie mix to butter; beat until well blended and crumbly.

3. Press ⅔ of crumb mixture onto bottom of ungreased 13×9-inch baking pan. Bake 15 minutes; let cool 5 minutes on wire rack.

4. Place pie filling in food processor; process until smooth. Stir in almond extract.

5. Pour filling mixture over crust. Sprinkle remaining crumb mixture evenly over filling. Return pan to oven; bake 20 to 25 minutes or until topping is golden and filling is slightly bubbly. Cool completely on wire rack. *Makes 2½ dozen bars*

# Super Chocolate Cookie Mix

- 1½ cups all-purpose flour
- 1 cup packed light brown sugar
- ¾ cup candy-coated chocolate pieces
- ½ cup salted peanuts, coarsely chopped
- ½ cup raisins
- ¼ cup unsweetened cocoa powder
- ¾ teaspoon baking soda
- ¼ teaspoon salt

**1.** Layer ingredients attractively in any order into 1-quart food storage jar with tight-fitting lid. Pack ingredients down slightly before adding another layer.

**2.** Cover top of jar with fabric; attach gift tag with raffia or ribbon.

*Makes one 1-quart jar*

## Super Chocolate Cookies

- ⅔ cup butter, softened
- 2 eggs
- 1½ teaspoons vanilla
- 1 jar Super Chocolate Cookie Mix

**1.** Preheat oven to 350°F.

**2.** Beat butter in large bowl until smooth. Beat in eggs and vanilla until blended. (Mixture may appear curdled.) Add cookie mix to butter mixture; stir until well blended.

**3.** Drop heaping tablespoonfuls dough 2 inches apart onto ungreased cookie sheets. Bake 11 to 12 minutes or until almost set. Let cookies stand on cookie sheets 2 minutes. Remove cookies to wire racks to cool completely. *Makes 2 dozen cookies*

# Fabulous Blondies Mix

- 1¾ cups all-purpose flour
- 1½ cups packed light brown sugar
- 1 cup (6 ounces) white chocolate chips
- 1 cup (4 ounces) blanched whole almonds, coarsely chopped
- 1 cup toffee baking pieces
- 1 teaspoon baking powder
- ¼ teaspoon salt

**1.** Layer ingredients attractively in any order into 1½-quart food storage jar with tight-fitting lid. Pack ingredients down slightly before adding another layer.

**2.** Cover top of jar with fabric; attach gift tag with raffia or ribbon.

*Makes one 1½-quart jar*

# Fabulous Blondies

- ⅔ cup butter, softened
- 2 eggs
- 2 teaspoons vanilla
- 1 jar Fabulous Blondies Mix

**1.** Preheat oven to 350°F. Lightly grease 13×9-inch baking pan.

**2.** Beat butter in large bowl until smooth. Beat in eggs and vanilla until blended. (Mixture may appear curdled.) Add blondie mix to butter mixture; stir until well blended.

**3.** Spread batter evenly in prepared pan. Bake 30 to 35 minutes or until golden brown. Cool in pan on wire rack.

*Makes 2½ dozen blondies*

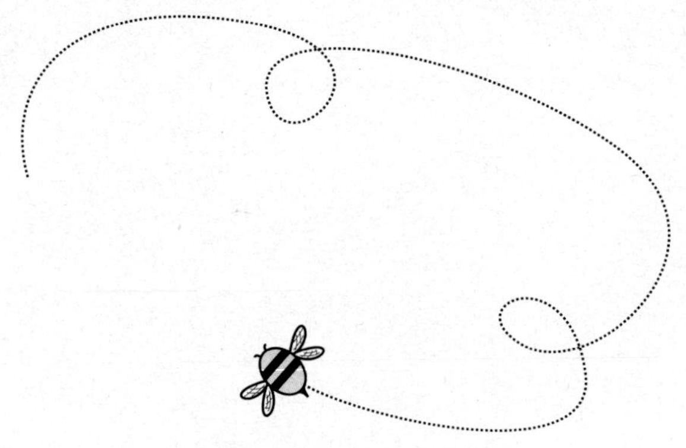

## Ultimate Chippers Mix

1¼ cups all-purpose flour
½ cup packed light brown sugar
½ cup semisweet chocolate chips
½ cup milk chocolate chips
½ cup white chocolate chips
¼ cup granulated sugar
¼ cup coarsely chopped pecans
½ teaspoon baking soda
¼ teaspoon salt

**1.** Layer ingredients attractively in any order into 1-quart food storage jar with tight-fitting lid. Pack ingredients down slightly before adding another layer.

**2.** Cover top of jar with fabric; attach gift tag with raffia or ribbon.

*Makes one 1-quart jar*

# Ultimate Chippers

½ cup butter, softened
1 egg
1½ teaspoons vanilla
1 jar Ultimate Chippers Mix

**1.** Preheat oven to 375°F.

**2.** Beat butter in large bowl until smooth. Beat in egg and vanilla until blended. (Mixture may appear curdled.) Add cookie mix to butter mixture; stir until well blended.

**3.** Drop heaping teaspoonfuls dough 2 inches apart onto ungreased cookie sheets. Bake 10 to 12 minutes or until edges are golden brown. Let cookies stand on cookie sheets 2 minutes. Remove cookies to wire racks to cool completely. *Makes 4 dozen cookies*

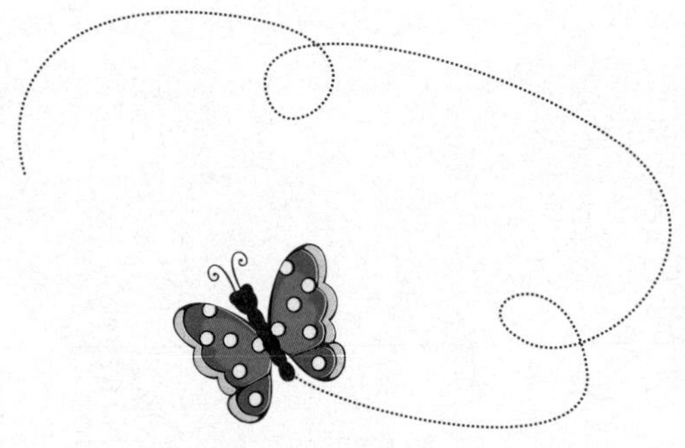

# METRIC CONVERSION CHART

## VOLUME MEASUREMENTS (dry)

1/8 teaspoon = 0.5 mL
1/4 teaspoon = 1 mL
1/2 teaspoon = 2 mL
3/4 teaspoon = 4 mL
1 teaspoon = 5 mL
1 tablespoon = 15 mL
2 tablespoons = 30 mL
1/4 cup = 60 mL
1/3 cup = 75 mL
1/2 cup = 125 mL
2/3 cup = 150 mL
3/4 cup = 175 mL
1 cup = 250 mL
2 cups = 1 pint = 500 mL
3 cups = 750 mL
4 cups = 1 quart = 1 L

## VOLUME MEASUREMENTS (fluid)

1 fluid ounce (2 tablespoons) = 30 mL
4 fluid ounces (1/2 cup) = 125 mL
8 fluid ounces (1 cup) = 250 mL
12 fluid ounces (1 1/2 cups) = 375 mL
16 fluid ounces (2 cups) = 500 mL

## WEIGHTS (mass)

1/2 ounce = 15 g
1 ounce = 30 g
3 ounces = 90 g
4 ounces = 120 g
8 ounces = 225 g
10 ounces = 285 g
12 ounces = 360 g
16 ounces = 1 pound = 450 g

## DIMENSIONS

1/16 inch = 2 mm
1/8 inch = 3 mm
1/4 inch = 6 mm
1/2 inch = 1.5 cm
3/4 inch = 2 cm
1 inch = 2.5 cm

## OVEN TEMPERATURES

250°F = 120°C
275°F = 140°C
300°F = 150°C
325°F = 160°C
350°F = 180°C
375°F = 190°C
400°F = 200°C
425°F = 220°C
450°F = 230°C

## BAKING PAN SIZES

| Utensil | Size in Inches/Quarts | Metric Volume | Size in Centimeters |
|---|---|---|---|
| Baking or Cake Pan (square or rectangular) | 8×8×2 | 2 L | 20×20×5 |
| | 9×9×2 | 2.5 L | 23×23×5 |
| | 12×8×2 | 3 L | 30×20×5 |
| | 13×9×2 | 3.5 L | 33×23×5 |
| Loaf Pan | 8×4×3 | 1.5 L | 20×10×7 |
| | 9×5×3 | 2 L | 23×13×7 |
| Round Layer Cake Pan | 8×1½ | 1.2 L | 20×4 |
| | 9×1½ | 1.5 L | 23×4 |
| Pie Plate | 8×1¼ | 750 mL | 20×3 |
| | 9×1¼ | 1 L | 23×3 |
| Baking Dish or Casserole | 1 quart | 1 L | — |
| | 1½ quart | 1.5 L | — |
| | 2 quart | 2 L | — |

*Delight family and friends with a thoughtful gift straight from your kitchen—a cookie, bar or brownie mix beautifully layered in a jar. With this unique book you'll have 15 recipes for pretty jars filled with the ingredients to bake delicious treats, as well as fun gift tags to attach to the jars. Gift giving has never been so easy!*

Manufactured in China.

ISBN 1-4127-2098-2